WEATHER AWARE

FLOODS
BE AWARE AND PREPARE

by Renée Gray-Wilburn

Consultant:
Joseph M. Moran, PhD
Meteorology, Professor Emeritus
University of Wisconsin-Green Bay

CAPSTONE PRESS
a capstone imprint

A+ Books are published by Capstone Press,
1710 Roe Crest Drive, North Mankato, Minnesota 56003
www.capstonepub.com

Library of Congress Cataloging-in-Publication Data
Gray-Wilburn, Renée.
  Floods : be aware and prepare / by Renée Gray-Wilburn ; editor, Jill Kalz.
      pages cm — (A+ books. Weather aware)
  Includes index.
  Summary: K-Grade 3.
  ISBN 978-1-4765-9904-5 (library binding)
  ISBN 978-1-4765-9909-0 (eBook PDF)
1. Floods—Juvenile literature. I. Kalz, Jill. II. Title.
  GB1399.G73 2015
  551.48'9—dc23   2014006230

Editorial Credits
Jill Kalz, editor; Lori Bye, designer; Svetlana Zhurkin, media researcher; Tori Abraham, production specialist

Photo Credits
Dreamstime: Inger Anne Hulbækdal, 19 (inset), Jan Wachala, 18–19, Rabbitsfoot, 26–27; Getty Images: Denver
Post, 16, 21, 28–29, DKP, cover; Newscom: dpa/picture-alliance/Jens Wolf, 11, Photoshot/Xinhua/Shariful
Islam, 13 (inset); Shutterstock: Alena Ozerova, 2 (middle left), 5, Andrew Zarivny, 1, Art Allianz, 3 (right),
23, Dan Schreiber, 2 (middle right), 6–7, Gina Jacobs, 3 (middle right), 17, Hal_P, 2 (left), 4, ivanovskyy, 8–9,
Kekyalyaynen, 2 (right), 10, Kuttelvaserova Stuchelova, 15, Mishella, 12–13, photka, 22, ronfromyork, cover
(inset), 3 (middle left), 24, Ryan Morgan, 9 (inset), Shabina Lourdes Dalidd, 3 (left), 20, sima, 14, Vitalijs Barisevs
(background), back cover and throughout

Note to Parents, Teachers, and Librarians
This Weather Aware book uses full-color photographs and a nonfiction format to introduce the concept of
floods. *Floods: Be Aware and Prepare* is designed to be read aloud to a pre-reader or to be read independently
by an early reader. Photographs help listeners and early readers understand the text and concepts discussed.
The book encourages further learning by including the following sections: Table of Contents, Critical Thinking
Using the Common Core, Glossary, Read More, Internet Sites, and Index. Early readers may need assistance
using these features.

Printed in the United States of America in North Mankato, Minnesota
032014   008087CGF14

TABLE OF CONTENTS

BE WEATHER AWARE

Weather usually follows a pattern. But once in a while, the pattern changes. To keep yourself safe, be weather aware. Here you'll learn about floods so you can better prepare for them.

WHAT IS A FLOOD?

Floods happen when a lot of water covers land that is normally dry.

Think of a cup. If you overfill it, it will run over. Lakes, rivers, and streams are like cups. They can hold only a certain amount of water. In a flood, extra water spills onto nearby land.

WHAT CAUSES FLOODS?

Most floods are caused by heavy rain falling in a short time. Strong storms may drop more than 2 inches (5 centimeters) of rain in an hour. Floods are also caused by quickly melting snow and ice.

Floods can happen when dams or levees break. These structures are built across rivers to hold back water. Older dams and levees may be weak. The extra water dumped by a storm may break them. In spring, blocks of river ice may act as a dam. When the ice breaks or shifts, too much water is released at once.

WHERE AND WHEN DO FLOODS HAPPEN?

Floods can happen almost anywhere. They usually happen near rivers and coasts. Valleys and canyons may flood when water flowing down nearby mountains fills them. Even deserts can flood. Their hard ground can't soak up heavy rains.

The country of Bangladesh floods more than anywhere else in the world. Flooding usually covers one-third of the country.

Floods happen most often during heavy rains. The land becomes too wet to absorb more water. Snowy winters can cause springtime flooding too. Ice and snow may melt too quickly for the frozen ground to absorb it.

WHY ARE FLOODS DANGEROUS?

When floodwater rises, it moves fast. It becomes a powerful force. It sweeps away anything in its path—cars, trees, and even buildings! Floods can destroy homes and land. People and animals may drown.

It takes only 6 inches (15 cm) of rushing floodwater to knock over an adult. Cars and pickups can be swept away in 2 feet (61 cm) of fast-moving water.

Floods also cause mudslides. Mudslides are common in areas with little plant cover. Rushing water washes rocks and dirt off hills. Floods often cut off power. With no power, towns may run out of food and clean water.

Most floods take days to build up. People have time to prepare. But flash floods form within hours of a heavy rain. Water races down mountains or out of streams without warning.

HOW DO YOU PREPARE FOR A FLOOD?

To prepare for a flood, plan ahead. Find the best paths to reach higher ground quickly and safely. Make an emergency kit. Pack it with food and water that will last for at least three days. Include first-aid supplies, a flashlight, batteries, a weather radio, and a blanket.

If a flood is likely, place sandbags in front of outside doors to help keep water out. Move anything of value to the highest floor of your house. If you are told to evacuate, leave right away.

WEATHER ALERTS

COASTAL FLOOD, FLASH FLOOD, OR FLOOD WATCH

Flooding is possible within the watch area.

COASTAL FLOOD, FLASH FLOOD, OR FLOOD WARNING

Flooding is happening or will happen soon within the warning area.

URBAN AND SMALL STREAM ADVISORY

Flooding of small streams, streets, and low-lying areas is happening or will happen soon.

During a flood, stay away from ditches and moving water. Get to higher ground as soon as possible. Never walk or drive through flooded areas. You won't know how deep the water is until it's too late.

Floods are a natural part of our world's weather. Thankfully, most are not very big or deadly. Knowing what to do before and during a flood will help keep you safe. Be weather aware!

CRITICAL THINKING USING THE COMMON CORE

1. Describe specific events that may trigger a flood. (Key Ideas and Details)

2. Describe how floods can be dangerous. (Craft and Structure)

3. Explain the differences between a flood watch, a flood warning, and an urban and small stream advisory, based on the chart on page 25. (Key Ideas and Details)

4. Explain the steps you would take at your home to prepare for a flood. (Integration of Knowledge and Ideas)

GLOSSARY

absorb (ab-ZORB)—to soak up

canyon (KAN-yuhn)—a deep, narrow area with steep sides; a canyon often has a stream or river running through it

dam (DAM)—a wall that stretches across a river; it slows down the rushing water and raises the water level behind it

evacuate (i-VA-kyuh-wayt)—to leave a place because of danger

flash flood (FLASH FLUHD)—a flood that happens with little or no warning, often during periods of heavy rainfall

levee (LEV-ee)—a bank built up near a river to keep it from flooding

READ MORE

Coster, Patience. *Rain and Floods.* Weatherwise. New York: PowerKids Press, 2010.

Gonzales, Doreen. *Floods and Tsunamis.* Killer Disasters. New York: PowerKids Press, 2013.

Koponen, Libby. *Floods.* A True Book. New York: Children's Press, 2009.

INTERNET SITES

FactHound offers a safe, fun way to find Internet sites related to this book. All of the sites on FactHound have been researched by our staff.

Here's all you do:

Visit *www.facthound.com*

Type in this code: 9781476599045

 Check out projects, games and lots more at **www.capstonekids.com**

INDEX